O

MW00527355

OUR
FATHER

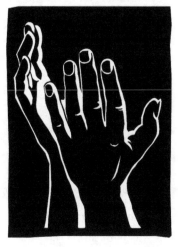

Alexander Schmemann

Translated by Alexis Vinogradov

ST VLADIMIR'S SEMINARY PRESS

Library of Congress Cataloging-in-Publication Data

Schmemann, Alexander, 1921–1983.
    [Otche nash. English]
    Our Father / Alexander Schmemann; translated by Alexis
Vinogradov,
        p. cm.
        ISBN 0–88141–234–1
        1. Lord's Prayer. I. Title.
BV230 .S3413 2002
226.9'606–dc2

2001057710

COPYRIGHT © 2000 BY
ST VLADIMIR'S SEMINARY PRESS
575 Scarsdale Road, Yonkers, NY 10707
1-800-204-2665
www.svspress.com

ISBN 0–88141–234–5

First printed 2002, reprinted 2003, 2014, 2018
Book illustration, design and cover by Amber Schley

Contents

Introduction

This commentary on The Lord's Prayer is actually a series of short broadcasts made by Father Alexander Schmemann on Radio Liberty to reach listeners in the former Soviet Union. This explains his frequent citation of noted Russian writers on one hand, and the concerns and approaches of agnostics, unbelievers, and militant atheists on the other. We are also made aware of his forceful indictment of a religion, or rather "religiosity," as he says, which is mired in itself with no reference to its ultimate goals and *raison d'etre*. This is the great "temptation" of faith turned into a comfortable and comforting religion in political conditions of both oppression and freedom. In lifting up this simplest and only "official" prayer given by Christ to the world, in his own simple yet profound style, he reminds us of what was lost in the centuries of this prayer's recitation, the apparent bankruptcy and irrelevance in our time of the timeless expressions in this prayer: *thy kingdom, thy will, daily bread, sin, forgiveness, temptation . . .*

If we are hoping for a soothing bedside meditation, we will be disappointed, as we find ourselves more awake and even jolted into an entirely new way of hearing those familiar petitions. If we are honest, we will of course find ourselves implicated in the many misunderstandings and distortions that have visited those enduring words over two millennia, and so, these reflections will be for us a welcome conversion. Because this single short prayer of Christ is cosmical, has everything that needs to be said about God, his kingdom, this life, about all of us—it is not an exaggeration to suggest that in this commentary, by thoroughly returning us to the essence of the Lord's Prayer, Father Schmemann has provided us with a map for seeing fresh and anew, the purpose and measure of our whole life!

In his writing and talks Father Alexander has frequently made the disclaimer that it is difficult, if not impossible, to convey certain theological understandings and perceptions of faith through words. Yet among those who have succeeded in painting verbal icons of life's mysteries and God's revelations, surely Father Alexander must be counted as a master, and so any effort at translation owes him an apology for what has diminished in passing

OUR FATHER

from his native and precise Russian into the present English translation. But this nevertheless remains a powerful gift, and since all good gifts are ultimately from the "Father of lights," may his divine light illumine the lines of these pages for each reader open to receive them.

In gratitude,
Alexis Vinogradov, translator

Our Father who art in heaven

J esus Christ left us only one prayer, which is therefore usually called the Lord's Prayer. When the disciples implored him, "Teach us to pray" (Lk 11.1), he gave them this prayer in reply:

Our Father who art in heaven,
Hallowed be thy name.
Thy kingdom come.
Thy will be done,
On earth as it is in heaven.
Give us this day our daily bread;
And forgive us our trespasses,
As we forgive those who trespass
   against us;
And lead us not into temptation,
But deliver us from evil.
(Mt 6.9–13)

This prayer has been said without interruption for two thousand years. At every moment somewhere on the globe people are saying those very words that were once uttered by Christ himself. This is why we have no better path to the very heart of Christianity than by this short, and on first observation simple, prayer. Albeit, it seems this prayer is not so simple since I have more than once been asked to explain it.

Let me begin this explanation by saying directly that its meaning is inexhaustible, that it is impossible to give this prayer one final and conclusive explanation. As with the Gospels, the Lord's Prayer is always addressed to each of us personally anew, in a way that makes it seem to have been composed specifically for me, for my needs, for my questions, for my pilgrimage. Yet, at the same time it remains eternal and unchanging in its essence, always calling us to what is most important, to the ultimate, to the highest.

In order to really hear the Lord's Prayer and participate in it, it is first necessary to rid ourselves of that inner confusion, that fragmentation of our attention, that spiritual sloppiness in which we constantly live. Possibly our most horrible trait is that we regularly hide from everything that seems too exalted and spiritually meaningful. It's as if we unconsciously choose to be petty and trivial, a choice easier to live by. (You might recall Tolstoy's character Svyazhsky in *Anna Karenina*, who seemed able to understand and discuss anything, but as soon as the conversation turned to deeper questions about the meaning of life, something in him shut down, and no one could penetrate this barrier. Tolstoy describes it with particular genius).

Indeed, so much of our inner strength is directed at stifling this inner voice, which calls us to an encounter with the ultimate.

And so, we must exercise at least some minimal effort to enter that framework, that state of spirit and soul in which this prayer of all prayers begins to sound, to resonate with us, and is revealed in its full meaning and becomes the one thing needed—food and drink for the soul.

So, let us lift up our minds and begin. Let us start with the salutation, which is at the same time both an appeal and an affirmation: "Our Father."

The first thing Christ offers to those who ask him to teach them to pray, the very first thing he leaves them as a priceless gift and consolation, as joy and inspiration, is the possibility of calling God "Father," to regard him as their father.

How many ideas have evolved in man's imagination about God! He has been referred to as the Absolute, the First Cause, Lord, Omnipotent, Creator, Benefactor, God, and so on, and so forth. Each of these ideas and designations relates to some element of truth, to a profound experience and a depth of understanding. Yet this one word "Father," together with "Our," contain all these concepts yet at the same time reveals them as intimacy, as love, as a unique, unrepeatable and joyful union.

"Our Father"—here we find the meaning of love and the answer to love; here lies the experience of intimacy and the joy of this experience; here faith opens into trust, and dependence yields to freedom, intimacy, and ultimately unfolds as joy. This is no longer an idea about God, but already knowledge of God, this is already communion with him in love, in unity, and trust. This is already the beginning of knowing eternity. For Christ himself said to the Father: "For this is eternal life, that they would know you" (Jn 17.3).

This salutation is therefore not only the beginning but the very foundation of the prayer; it renders all the other petitions possible and fills them with meaning. In its deepest and original sense Christianity is the *religion of fatherhood*, which means that it is not founded on intellectual ideals or philosophical deductions, but on the experience of love that floods our whole life, on the experience of *personal* love.

All of this is implied within the initial appeal of the Lord's Prayer: "Our Father." Having uttered these words, we add: "who art in heaven." And here the whole prayer (and with it our whole life) is lifted up, is raised to heaven, for heaven is, after all, that vertical dimension of life, that reference of man to the higher and spiritual, which is at the same time the object of such hatred and mockery among those who reduce human life to purely biological and material categories.

This is not the physical or astronomical heaven that is always refuted by atheists, but it is rather the highest pole of human life: "the

Father who is in heaven." This is the faith of man in the divine love that embraces and permeates the whole world. And this is faith in the world as the reflection, the sign, the presence of this love; this is faith in heaven as the ultimate vocation of man's glory and destiny, as his eternal home.

The joyful affirmation and herald of all this is the opening of that prayer that Christ gave us as the sign of our divine sonship: "Our Father, who art in heaven."

Hallowed be thy name

Following the joyful, festive, and loving salutation, "Our Father, who art in heaven," we say, "hallowed be thy name." What are we praying, what are we asking, what need are we expressing as we pronounce these words?

What does it mean to hallow the name of God?

I am convinced, alas, that most of the faithful who pronounce these words do not really contemplate their meaning. For atheists, this is just one more excuse to shrug their shoulders to the confusing and mystical combination of words: "hallowed be thy name."

From earliest times man called sacred or holy that which he perceived as the supreme value, demanding reverence, acknowledgment, awe, and thanksgiving; which at the same time attracted man to itself, inspiring familiarity and intimacy. We speak of the sacred feeling of homeland, of the sacred love towards parents, of sacred awe in the face of beauty, perfection, wonder. Thus, the sacred is that which is higher, purer, demanding all that is best: the best sentiments, the best efforts, the best hopes in man. The peculiarity of the sacred is precisely in the fact that it demands from us an inner awareness of self-evident and free desires; yet not simply an awareness, but action and life consistent with this awareness. The awareness that two times two makes four, or that water boils at a specific temperature leaves us neither better nor worse; such an awareness belongs to the righteous and the unrighteous, to the ignorant and the intelligent, the genius and the simpleton. But if we experience a sacred awareness in terms of beauty, or moral perfection, or a special intuition about the world and life, then this awareness immediately makes some demand on us, effects some change in us, invites us somewhere, captivates us, seduces us.

How simply and beautifully Pushkin described this in his famous poem, "The memory of a glorious moment. . . ." The poet forgets the "vision," the intrusion of "disturbing storms," the dispersion of "previous hopes," and writes,

> . . . my soul was stirred
> and once again you came,
> a passing vision,
> a glimmer of beauty pure
> In fullness beats my heart,
> feeling once again
> the resurrection of divinity,
> and inspiration, and life,
> and tears, and love.

Here is a description of the sacred as beauty. This experience changes life in its entirety, fills it, in the words of Pushkin, with meaning, and inspiration, and joy, and the divine.

Religious experience is the experience of the holy in its purest form. Whoever has some measure of this experience knows that it penetrates one's whole life, demanding a change and an inner transformation. But he knows as well that this desire is also blocked by a certain inertia, a weakness, the pettiness of our existence and, above all, by that almost instinctive fear of man in the face of the sacred—that is, the highest, the pure, and divine. Our hearts and souls feel literally wounded by this encounter with the holy, and we are inspired to align our whole being with this desire. But then we are reminded by the Apostle Paul that inside ourselves there is a law that fights against this very desire (Rom 7.23).

"Hallowed be thy name"—this is the cry of the one who has seen and recognized God, and knows that only in this vision and encounter can he find the fullness of life, full inspiration, and full happiness.

"Hallowed be thy name"—may everything in the world, beginning with my own life, my deeds, my words be a reflection of this sacred and divine name, which has been revealed and given to us. May life once more become an ascension towards the light, an exaltation, praise, the power of good. May everything be filled with divine wisdom and divine love.

"Hallowed be thy name"—this is also a petition for help in the difficult effort in this ascension and transformation, for we are surrounded and held captive to darkness, evil, pettiness, superficiality, turmoil. Each ascent is vanquished by a fall, each effort followed by such an attack of weakness and despondency that in the words of the writer Fyodor Tyutchev: "life is like a wounded bird that tries to ascend but can't . . ."

The experience of the holy is a mystical "encounter with worlds beyond," a "fleeting vision of pure beauty," which makes life not easier but, in fact, harder, and one begins to envy people who are simply immersed in the fuss and bother of life with no inner struggle. However, it is precisely in this struggle that man fulfills his high vocation, only here in this effort, in these ascents and descents, can he consider himself a person.

All of this is implied in that first petition of the Lord's Prayer. Such a short yet simultaneously joyful and difficult petition: "Hallowed be thy name."

All of what is best in me is capable not only of pronouncing these words, but also of profoundly living by them; everything in me seeks that new life, a life that would shine and burn with a holy flame, consuming all impurity, all unworthy visions that drag me down. My Lord, what an arduous petition, what a burden Christ laid upon us in giving it to us, in showing us that this is the only worthy prayer to God, and as such, must be our

31

very first prayer! How rarely we pronounce these words, acknowledging all this, and yet how good it is that we repeat them again and again. For it is only while these words, "Hallowed be thy name," remain heard in the world, while they are not forgotten, that man will not be entirely depersonalized, that he will not totally betray the vocation for which he was created by God.

"Hallowed be thy name."

Thy kingdom come

The second petition of the Lord's Prayer is: "Thy kingdom come." As with the first petition, we must ask what meaning does a believing Christian ascribe to these words; to what does he direct his conscience, his hope, his

desire? I am afraid that, as with the first petition, this question is equally hard to answer.

At the dawn of Christianity the meaning of
this petition was simple, or more accurately,
one can say that it embodied and expressed
the essential in Christian faith and hope. For
it is enough to read the Gospels once to be
convinced that the teaching of the kingdom
of God lies at the very heart of the preaching
and teaching of Christ. Christ came preaching
the gospel of the kingdom, saying: "Repent,
for the kingdom of heaven is at hand" (Mt
4.17). Almost all of Christ's parables concern
the kingdom. He compares it to the treasure
for which the man sells all he has; to the seed
from which grows an enormous tree; to the
yeast that leavens the whole lump of dough.

Throughout we hear this mystical yet alluring
promise, this announcement, this invitation

into the kingdom of God. "Seek first the kingdom of God" (Mt 6.33), that you may be "sons of the kingdom" (Mt 13.38). So, possibly the most amazing fact in the long history of Christianity is that this core and central understanding, this very nucleus of the gospel message, confronts us now as a new riddle, whose answer was lost along the way. But how are we to pray about the kingdom of God, how are we to say to God and to ourselves, "Thy kingdom come," if in fact these words elude us?

The difficulty here lies first in the fact that the Gospel itself seems to give the kingdom a double meaning. On the one hand it seems to refer to the future, to the end, to the beyond; it seems to refer to that for which its opponents, the atheists, have always chided Christianity—that Christianity seems to have its center of gravity in some other invisible world beyond the grave, and therefore remains unmoved by the evil and injustice of this world, that Christianity is simply a religion of another world. If that's the case, then the petition, "Thy kingdom come," is a prayer for the end of the world, of its disappearance, a prayer specifically for the hastening of precisely this remote world beyond the grave.

But then why does Christ say that the kingdom has arrived, and to his disciples' questions he replies that the kingdom is among them and within them? Doesn't this mean that we can't define the kingdom simply in terms of a different future world coming after a catastrophic end and annihilation of this earthly world?

It is here that we begin approaching the central issue. For if we have ceased to understand the gospel of the kingdom, and no longer know what we pray when saying the words of the Lord's Prayer, "Thy kingdom come," it is because we no longer hear them in their fullness. We always start with ourselves, with questions about ourselves, for even the so-called "believer" is very often interested in religion insofar as it answers questions concerning himself: is my soul immortal, does death put an end to everything or is there possibly something there beyond that fearful and mysterious leap into the unknown?

But the Gospel does not speak about such things. It calls "kingdom" the encounter of man with God, God who is fullness of life and the very life of all life, who is light, love, knowledge, wisdom, eternity. It tells us that the kingdom comes and begins when man meets God, recognizes him, and with love and joy offers himself to him. It says that the kingdom of God comes when my life is filled to the brim with this light, with this knowledge, with this love. And finally it says for the person who has experienced this encounter and has filled his life with this divine life, that everything, including his death, is revealed in a new light, for that which he encounters, that with which he fills his life here and now, today, is eternity itself, which is God himself.

Indeed, what are we praying for when we pronounce these absolutely unique words, "Thy kingdom come"? Above all, of course, we pray that this encounter may take place now, here, and today, in the present circumstances, that in my mundane and difficult life I could hear the words, "the kingdom is near you," and that my life would be filled with the power and light of the kingdom, with the power and light of faith, love, and hope. Furthermore, we desire that the whole world, which so evidently lies in evil and longing, in fear and in striving, would see and receive this light, which entered the world some two thousand years ago, when at the outskirts of the Roman empire was heard that lonely, yet still resounding voice: "Repent, for the kingdom of God is at hand" (Mt 3.2). We pray also that God would help us to not betray this kingdom, not to constantly fall away from it, not to sink into the engulfing darkness, and that finally, this kingdom of God would come in power, as Christ says.

Yes, Christianity always contains the anticipation of the future, anticipation of the beloved, hope for the final manifestation on earth and in heaven: "that God may be everything to everyone" (1 Cor 15.28), "Thy kingdom come." In a sense it isn't even a prayer; rather it is the heartbeat of anyone who has at least once in his life seen, felt, loved the light and joy of God's kingdom and who knows that it is the

beginning, the content, and the fulfillment of
everything that lives.

C H A P T E R 4

Thy will be done
on earth as it is in heaven

T hy will be done on earth as it is in heaven" (Mt 6.10). Here is the third petition of the Lord's Prayer.

Of all of them this petition seems to be the simplest and most understandable. Indeed, if a person believes in God, it would seem he submits to God's will and accepts it, and desires that it should be accepted all around him, on earth, as supposedly it is in heaven. In reality, however, this is the most difficult petition.

I would have to say that precisely this petition, "Thy will be done" is the ultimate yardstick of faith, the measure by which one can discern, in oneself first of all, profound from superficial faith, profound religiosity from a false one. Why? Well, because even the most ardent believer all too regularly, if not always, desires, expects, and asks from the God he claims to believe in that God would fulfill precisely his own will and not the will of God. The best proof of this is the Gospel itself, the account of Christ's life.

Isn't Christ from the outset followed by nameless crowds of people? And aren't they following him because he is accomplishing their will? He is healing, helping, comforting . . . However, as soon as he starts speaking about the essential, about the fact that a person has to deny himself if he wants to follow him, about the need to love one's enemies, and to lay down one's life for one's brothers, as soon as his teaching becomes difficult, exalted, a call to sacrifice, a demand of the impossible—in other words, as soon as Christ starts to teach about what is the will of God, people immediately abandon him and, moreover, turn against him with anger and hatred. This eerie shouting of the mob at the Cross, "Crucify him, crucify him!" (Lk 23.21)—is it not because Christ did not fulfill the will of the people?

They only wanted help and healing, while he spoke of love and forgiveness. They wanted him to liberate them from their enemies and grant victory over them, while he spoke of the kingdom of God. They wanted him to observe their traditions and customs, while he defied them by eating and drinking with publicans, sinners, and harlots. Doesn't the root and cause of Judas' betrayal lie precisely in this disappointment in Christ? Judas anticipated that Christ would fulfill his will, but Christ willingly gave himself to judgment and death.

This is all described in the Gospels. And subsequently, over the next two millennia of Christianity, do we not witness the same drama? What do we together and individually really desire from Christ? Let's admit it— the fulfillment of *our* will. We desire that God would assure our happiness. We want him to defeat our enemies. We want him to realize our dreams and that he would consider us kind and good. And when God fails to do our will, we are frustrated and upset, and are ready over and over to forsake and deny him.

"Thy will be done"—but in fact we are thinking: "Our will be done," and thus this third petition of the Lord's Prayer is first of all a kind of judgment on us, a judgment of our faith.

Do we really desire that which is from God? Do we really desire to accept that difficult, exalted, that seemingly impossible demand of the Gospel? And this petition also becomes a kind of verification of our goals and directions in life: what is it that I want, what is it that forms the main and highest value of my life; where is that treasure about which Christ said that where it lies, there our hearts will be also (Mt 6.21)?

If the history of religion, if the history of Christianity is filled with betrayals, then these betrayals are not so much in the sins and failures of people, for the sinner can always repent, the failure can always correct himself, the ailing can always be restored. No, rather the worst betrayal lies in this constant substitution of our will, our selfwill, for the will of God. On account of this betrayal even religion becomes our egoism, which therefore deserves the accusations it endures from its enemies. It becomes a pseudo-religion, and there is nothing on the face of the earth more frightening than pseudo-religion. For it is precisely pseudo-religion that killed Christ.

It was those who considered themselves most deeply religious who condemned him to death and crucified him, who mocked him and sought his destruction. Some of them perceived in religion a kind of national apotheosis, for whom Christ was a danger-ous revolutionary who talked of love for one's enemies; others saw in religion only the miraculous and powerful, for whom the bloody and helpless Christ hanging on the cross was a disgrace to religion; while still others were disappointed in him because he taught things they did not want to hear. And so to this day people continue to think the same way, which underlines the importance of this petition, "Thy will be done."

"Thy will be done." This means first of all: grant me strength and help me to understand what your will is, help me to overcome the limitations of my own reasoning, of my heart, my own will, in order to discern your paths, even if they are unclear at first. Help me to accept that which is difficult and seemingly unbearable or impossible in your will. Help me, in other words, to desire that which you desire.

And here begins this narrow path spoken of by Christ. No sooner do we begin desiring this divine will, this high and difficult calling, than people immediately turn from us, our friends betray us, and we are left alone, persecuted and ostracized. But this is always a sign that a person has accepted the will of God, and it is always a promise that this narrow and difficult path is crowned with victory—not a passing human victory, but victory from God.

Give us this day our daily bread

"Give us this day our daily bread" (Mt 6.11). This is the fourth petition—the one concerning our daily bread. The word daily really means "substantive," that which is essential for survival, which is why we need it as daily food. If the first three petitions related directly to God, if they expressed our desire that his name would be glorified, that his kingdom would come, that his will would be accomplished not only in heaven but on earth as well; then with this fourth petition we are, as it were, switching over to our own needs, we begin to pray for ourselves. The bread signifies here not only bread as such, and not even food in general, but absolutely everything necessary for life, everything that makes possible our existence.

In order to get to the heart of this petition, it is important to recall everything related to the symbol of food in the Bible, for only there does this petition cease to have a limited relation to the strictly physical side of man's life and is disclosed in its fullness.

We find the meaning of food in the very first chapter of the Bible, in the account of the creation of man. Having created the world, God gives it as food for man, and this means first of all that man's life depends on food— that is, on the world. Man lives by food, transforms food into his own life. This dependency of man on the external, on matter, on the world is so self-evident, that Feuerbach, one of the founders of materialist philosophy, consigned man into the famous formula: "man is what he eats." But the teaching and revelation of the Bible does not rest on this dependency. Man receives food—that is, life itself—from God. It is God's gift to man, and he lives not in order to eat and thereby maintain his physiological survival, but in order to develop in himself the image and likeness of God.

Thus, food itself became the gift of life as the knowledge of the freedom and the beauty of the spirit. Food is transformed into life, but food is revealed from the outset as the victory over this dependency on food alone, for in creating man God commands him to have dominion over the earth. Therefore, in receiving food from God as the gift of God, man is filled with divine life itself. This is why the biblical account of the fall of man is linked with food.

This is the famous story of the forbidden fruit, which man ate secretly apart from God, in order to become like God. The meaning of this account is simple: man believed that from food alone, that by pure reliance on its consumption, he could receive that which is actually possible to receive only from God. By way of food he sought liberation from God, which only led him to slavery and dependence on food; man became a slave of the world. But this also means a slave of death, for the food that gives him his physical life cannot give him that freedom from the world and death, which can only come from God.

Give us this day our daily bread

Food, the symbol and source of life, became the symbol of death. For if a man does not eat, he dies. But if he eats, he still dies, for food itself is a communion with that which has died and, therefore, with death. And so, finally, salvation, and recreation, and forgiveness, and resurrection itself are linked also in the Gospel with food.

When Christ was tempted in the wilderness by the devil and felt hunger, the devil suggested that he turn the stones into bread, but Christ refused saying: "Man does not live by bread alone" (Mt 4.4). He overcame and judged that very dependency of man on bread alone, on the physical life, which became the burden, in the biblical symbolism, of the first man. He freed himself from this dependency, and food became once more the gift of God, communion with the divine life, with freedom and eternity, and not slavery to the mortal world.

This is the profound meaning of that new divine food, which constitutes from the earliest days of Christianity the main joy, the chief mystery of the Church that Christians call the Eucharist, which means "thanksgiving." The Eucharist, faith in participation in the new food, in the new and heavenly bread, fulfills the Christian revelation about food. And only in the light of this revelation, of the joy of this thanksgiving, can one adequately understand the full depth of this fourth petition of the Lord's Prayer: "Give us this day our daily bread." Give us, today, the food that is essential for us.

Naturally, in the first instance these are things basic to life: bread, food, air, all that which becomes our life. But this is not all. "(You) Give us": this means that the ultimate source of all this for us is God himself, his love, his concern for us; in whatever form or from whomever we may receive the gift, all is from him. But this means that the first meaning and goal of these gifts is God himself.

We receive bread, we receive life, but in order that the purpose of this life may be revealed. And the purpose of this life lies in God, in knowledge of him, in love for him, in communion with him, in the joy of his eternity, and in that life that the Gospel calls "life in abundance" (Jn 10.10).

My Lord, how remote is this understanding from the philosophy of that insignificant and blind guide named Feuerbach. Of course, as he said, man is what he eats. But what he eats is the gift of God's love; what he participates in is light and glory and joy, and living he lives by everything that God gives him.

"Give us this day ..." In your love, give us all this today, give us not simply to exist, but to truly love that full, meaningful, and profoundly divine and eternal life, for which you created us, which you gave us and which you always give us, and in which we come to know, love, and give thanks to you.

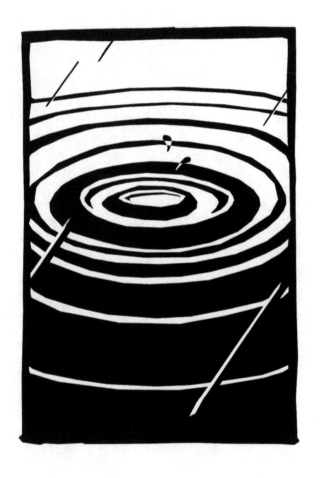

*And forgive us our trespasses
as we forgive those who trespass
against us*

"And forgive us our trespasses as we forgive those who trespass against us" (Mt 6.12). Let us notice at the outset that this petition directly unites two acts: the forgiveness of our sins by

God is connected to our forgiveness of sins committed against us. Christ says: "If you forgive men their trespasses, your heavenly Father also will forgive you; but if you do not forgive men their trespasses, neither will your Father forgive your trespasses" (Mt 6.14–15). And, of course, precisely here in this connection, in this relationship lies the profound mystery of forgiveness in the Lord's Prayer.

But before we consider this connection, it is essential to look at how one understands sin, for it has become a foreign concept for contemporary man. He knows the idea of crime, which is primarily related to the breaking of a given law. The concept of crime is relative. So, for example, a crime in one country may not be a crime in another. For if there is no law, there is no crime. Crime is not only related to the law, but in some measure arises out of the law. But the law, in its turn, arises out of societal needs. It has no connection, and cannot have one, to that which goes on in the depths of man's consciousness. As long as a person does not violate the peaceful life of society and does not cause any obvious harm to others or to established customs, there is no crime, as there is also no law. Hatred, for example, cannot be the substance of a crime until it has resulted in some action: physical harm, murder, or theft. On the other hand, the law does not know forgiveness, for the very purpose of the law is to defend and maintain order in human society—an order that depends on the functioning of the law.

That is why it is so important to understand that when we speak of *sin,* we are actually dealing with something categorically different by its very nature from the social conception of crime. If we know crime on the basis of the law, then sin is disclosed through conscience. If it is absent in us, if the understanding of conscience in human society diminishes, or better put, if the direct experience of conscience fades, then it follows that the religious conception of sin becomes vague and superfluous as does the related notion of forgiveness.

What is conscience? What is sin, to which our conscience testifies, and which it reveals? This isn't simply some inner voice, telling us what is good and what is bad. This isn't simply an innate ability to discern good from evil; it is rather something still deeper and more mystical. A man may find that he hasn't committed a wrong, has in no way contravened a law, did no harm to anyone, and yet have a troubled conscience.

A clean conscience, a guilty conscience—it is possible that these common expressions best convey the mystical nature of conscience. Dostoevsky's Ivan Karamazov knows that he did not kill his father. And yet he is equally convinced that he is guilty of the murder. Conscience is precisely this deep conviction of guilt, the awareness of one's implication, not in a crime or in some evil as such, but in that deep inner evil, in that moral depravity, out of which spring all the crimes on earth, before which all laws are helpless. And when Dostoevsky uttered his famous line about how "everybody is guilty before everyone and for all"—this wasn't simply rhetoric or an exaggeration, but a debilitating intuition of guilt, a truth of conscience. For it is not simply the case that we all to a greater or lesser degree transgress this or that law, that we are guilty of some great, or more often little, crimes; it is rather the case that we have accepted as a fact of life that inner division, that inner conflict among ourselves, that rupture of life, that mistrust, that absence of love and unity in which the world lives—this lie that our conscience discloses.

For the profound law of life consists not simply in doing no wrong, but in doing good, and this means first of all to accept the other, which means to effect that unity without which even the most law-abiding society still becomes a living hell. This is the essence of sin, and it is for the remission of this sin, the sin of all sins, that we pray in the fifth petition of the Lord's Prayer.

But to see all this as sin, to ask forgiveness of this sin, means to acknowledge our disunity with others, and it implies an effort to overcome it, which already implies its forgiveness. For forgiveness is a mystical action that restores a lost wholeness, so that goodness reigns once more; forgiveness is not a legal action, but a moral one. According to the law anyone who harms me must be punished, and until he is punished the law is not satisfied, but according to conscience the moral law does not require a legal satisfaction, but rather the restoration of wholeness and love, which any law is powerless to effect. Only mutual forgiveness has this power. If we forgive one another, then God forgives us, and only in this mutually related forgiveness of ours and the forgiveness from above is the conscience purified and light reigns. It is this for which man thirsts and searches at his very depths.

For indeed, man does not really need external order as much as a clean conscience, that inner light without which there can be no true happiness. Therefore, "forgive us our trespasses as we forgive those who trespass against us" is actually a petition for moral purification and rebirth, without which any law of this world is of no help.

Perhaps the terrible tragedy of our times, of those societies in which we live, consists precisely in the fact that while there is much talk about legality and justice, while many assorted texts are cited, these societies have almost entirely lost the power and moral beauty of forgiveness. This is why the petition in the Lord's Prayer for forgiveness of sins of those who have sinned against us, and of us and our sins by God, is possibly that very center of moral rebirth before which we stand in this age.

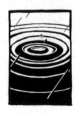

And lead us not into temptation
but deliver us from the evil one

The last petition of the Lord's Prayer reads: "And lead us not into temptation but deliver us from the evil one" (Mt 6.13). Quite early on this petition led to misunderstanding and was subjected to all sorts of interpretations.

First of all, what is the possible meaning of "lead us not"? Is it possible that God himself is responsible for tempting us, for sending us the sufferings, trials, temptations, and doubts that fill our life and so often make it unbearable? Or perhaps, does God torture us at least for the sake of our eventual illumination and salvation?

Furthermore, who is this "evil one" from whom we seek deliverance? This expression was and is often translated as simply "evil," while the Greek original, *apo tou ponirou*, can be translated as either "from the evil one" or "from evil."

In either case, what is the origin of this evil? If God truly exists, then why does evil triumph, and why do evil persons win? And why is the presence of evil power much more evident than the presence of God's power? If God exists, how does he permit all this? And if, let's say, God decides to save me, then why doesn't he save others around me who are dying and in such terrible suffering?

Let us admit that these questions cannot be readily answered. Or more precisely, these questions cannot be answered at all, if we seek an answer that has a rational, intelligent, so-called "objective" formulation. All attempts at theodicy—that is, the rational explanation for the existence of evil in the world in the presence of an al-lpowerful God have proven unsuccessful and unconvincing. One of the most forceful rebuttals of such explanations remains the famous answer of Dostoevsky's Ivan Karamazov: "If future happiness is built on the teardrop of even one child, I respect-fully return my ticket to such happiness."

But what then can be said?

Here one can begin to unravel the meaning, or perhaps more accurately, the inner power, of this last petition of the Lord's Prayer, "And lead us not into temptation but deliver us from the evil one." For, in the first instance, evil comes to us precisely as temptation, as doubt, as the disintegration of faith; the victory of darkness, cynicism, and helplessness in our soul.

The awesome force of evil does not lie in evil as such, but in its destruction of our faith in goodness—our conviction that good is stronger than evil. This is the meaning of temptation. And even the very attempt to explain evil by virtue of rational arguments, to legitimize it, if one can put it this way, is that very same temptation; it is the inner surrender before evil. For the Christian attitude towards evil consists precisely in the understanding that evil has no explanation, no justification, no basis; that it is the root of rebellion against

God, falling away from God, a rupture from full life; and that God does not give us explanations for evil, but strength to resist evil and power to overcome it. And again, this victory lies not in the ability to understand and explain evil but rather in the ability to face it with the full force of faith, the full force of hope, the full force of love. For it is by faith, hope, and love that temptations are overcome; they are the answer to temptation, the victory over temptations, and therefore the victory over evil.

Here lies the victory of Christ, the one whose whole life was one seamless temptation. He was constantly in the midst of evil in all its forms, beginning with the slaughter of innocent infants at the time of his birth and ending in horrible isolation, betrayal by all, physical torture, and an accursed death on the cross. In one sense the Gospels are an account of the power of evil and the victory over it—an account of Christ's temptation.

And Christ didn't once explain and therefore didn't once justify and legitimize evil, but he constantly confronted it with faith, hope, and love. He didn't destroy evil, but he did reveal the power of struggle with evil, and he gave this power to us; and it is about this power that we pray when we say: "And lead us not into temptation."

The Gospel says about Christ that when he was suffering alone, at night, in the garden, abandoned by all; when he "began to be sorrowful and troubled" (Mt 26.37); when all the force of temptation fell on him, an angel came from heaven and strengthened him.

It is about this same mystical assistance that we pray, so that in the face of evil, suffering, and temptation our faith would not waver, our hope not weaken, our love not dry up; that the darkness of evil not reign in our hearts and become itself the fuel for evil. Our prayer is that we can trust in God, as Christ trusted him, that all the temptations would be smashed against our strength.

We pray also that God would deliver us from the evil one, and here we are given not an explanation but one more revelation, this time about the *personal* nature of evil, about the person as the bearer and source of evil.

There exists no concrete reality that we could call hatred, but it appears in all its awesome power when there is one who hates; there is no suffering as such, but there is the sufferer; everything in this world, everything in this life is personal. Thus it is not from some impersonal evil, but rather from the evil *one* that we ask for deliverance in the Lord's Prayer. The source of evil is in the evil person, and this means in the person in whom paradoxically and horribly evil has replaced good, and who lives by evil. It is perhaps here, in these words about the evil one, that we are given the one possible explanation of evil, for here we discover that it is not some kind of impersonal force spread throughout the world, but rather as the tragedy of a personal choice, personal responsibility, personal decision.

And therefore only in the person, and not in abstract theories and arrangements, is evil defeated and goodness triumphs; which is why we pray first of all for ourselves, for each time that we overcome temptation, it is because we choose faith, hope, and love and not the gloom of evil.

A new order of causality is established in the world, a new possibility of triumph, heralded

by this prayer: "And lead us not into temptation but deliver us from the evil one."

For thine is the kingdom, the power, and the glory

With this conversation we end our brief, and far from adequate, explanation of the Lord's Prayer. We saw that behind each word, behind each petition, there lies a world of spiritual realities, spiritual connections that regularly escape our attention, that have vanished in the turmoil of our daily lives. From this point of view, the prayer, "Our Father," is more than a prayer; it is an epiphany and revelation of that spiritual world for which we are created, that hierarchy of values that enables us to arrange everything in its place within our lives. Each petition opens a whole layer of personal awareness, a whole revelation about our selves.

"Our Father, who art in heaven! Hallowed be thy Name." This means that my own life is referred to the highest, divine, absolute existence, and only within this reference does it find its meaning, its light, and its direction.

"Thy kingdom come." This means that my life is predestined to be filled with this kingdom of goodness, love, and joy; that my life should be permeated and illumined by the power of this kingdom that is opened and granted to us by God.

"Thy will be done on earth as it is in heaven." That I may judge and measure my life according to this will, that in it I may find an immutable moral law, that before it I may humble my selfwill, my egoism, my passions, my mindlessness.

"Give us this day our daily bread." That I might receive my entire life, all of its joys and also all of its sadness, all of its beauty yet also suffering, as a gift from the hand of God, with thanksgiving and awe. That I may live only by the most satisfying, the essential and highest, and not by those things by which the priceless gift of life is frittered away.

"And forgive us our trespasses, as we forgive those who trespass against us." That I may always be filled with the spirit of forgiveness, the desire to build my whole existence on love; that all my failings, all my debts, all the sins of my life may be covered by the bright forgiveness of God.

"And lead us not into temptation, but deliver us from the evil one." That in offering myself up to God's mystical and radiant will, with his help, I may overcome all temptation, and mainly the most terrible of all—the blindness that obscures and prevents the world and life from seeing the presence of God, and which steals life from God, rendering it blind and evil; that I would not yield to the force and charm of an evil person; that within me I would not harbor the ambiguity and perversion of evil that always masquerades as good, always taking the form of the angel of light.

And the Lord's Prayer ends with and is crowned with the solemn exclamation: "For thine is the kingdom and the power and the glory forever": three key words and biblical meanings, three main symbols of the Christian faith. The *kingdom*: "The kingdom of God is near" (Mt 4.17), "the kingdom of heaven is in the midst of you" (Lk 17.21), "Thy kingdom come"—is near, has come, is revealed—how?—in the life, in the words, in the teaching, in the death, and finally, in the Resurrection of Jesus Christ; in that life that is filled with such light and such power, in these words that lead us so high, in this teaching that answers all our questions, and finally, in that end with which everything started anew and which for us became the beginning of new life.

When we speak of the kingdom of God, moreover, we are not speaking about something abstract, not about some afterlife, not about something that will happen after death. We are speaking above all about something that was announced, promised, and given by Christ to those who believe in him and love him; and we call this the kingdom, because there has never been anything better, more beautiful, resplendent and joyful revealed, promised and given to people. This is the meaning of "For thine is the kingdom . . ."

". . . and the *power*," we continue further. What possible kind of power can one attribute to this person who died alone on the cross, never defending himself, and having "no place to lay his head" (Mt 8.20)? But just compare him to the strongest power on earth. Whatever power a man acquires, with whatever forces he surrounds himself, however he subjects others to himself, there comes the inevitable moment when all of it turns to dust and nothing remains of that power. But this one, this "weak" and "powerless" one, lives, and nothing, no power, can erase his memory from the consciousness of mankind. People leave him; they forget about him and then return again. They are seduced by other words, by other promises, but in the end, sooner or later, there remains only that small, very simple book and the words within it. From it radiates that image of the person who says: "For judgment I came into this world, that those who do not see may see, and that those who see may become blind" (Jn 9.39); who also said: "A new commandment I give to you, that you love one another" (Jn 13.34); and who said, finally: "I have overcome the world" (Jn 16.33). So, this is why we say to him: "For thine is the kingdom, and the power"—and finally, "*glory.*"

How illusory, brief, and fragile is any glory in this world. It seems that what Christ sought least of all was glory. But if there is any profound and indestructible glory, it is only the one that ignites and burns wherever he is—

the glory of goodness, the glory of faith, the glory of hope. He is first of all the one who suddenly becomes lightbearing, who himself radiates a light unknown on earth. And gazing upon him we understand the poet who exclaimed: "He speaks with the glory of the stars, and with the beauty of the first created day!"

We understand not with our intellect, but with our whole being, that which man seeks and thirsts for so passionately in all his turmoil and strife: he longs to be on fire with this light; he desires that everything would shine with this heavenly beauty, that everything would be filled with this divine glory.

"For thine is the kingdom, the power, and the glory forever." Thus ends the Lord's Prayer. And while we remember this prayer, while we keep repeating it, our life is opened toward the kingdom, is filled with power, shines with

For thine is the kingdom

glory, in the face of which darkness, hatred,
and evil lie powerless.

ABOUT THE AUTHOR

Father Alexander Schmemann was a prolific writer, brilliant lecturer, and dedicated pastor. Former dean and professor of liturgical theology at St Vladimir's Orthodox Seminary, he passed away in 1983 at the age of sixty-two. Father Alexander Schmemann's insight into contemporary culture, church life, and liturgical celebration left an indelible mark on the Christian community worldwide.

Printed in the USA
CPSIA information can be obtained
at www.ICGtesting.com
LVHW012219181223
766859LV00012B/718